WALRUSES

WALRUSES

CHARLES ROTTER

THE CHILD'S WORLD

PHOTO RESEARCH

Charles Rotter/Gary Lopez Productions

PHOTO CREDITS

Leonard Lee Rue III: front cover, 14, 23

Kathy Dawson: back cover

Lon E. Lauber/Aleutian Photographic: 2, 9, 21, 28, 31

Dana J. Seagars/U.S. Fish and Wildlife Service: 6, 13, 24

Thomas Mangelsen/Images of Nature: 10, 27

Tony Dawson: 17

Kathy Watkins/Images of Nature: 18

Distributed to schools and libraries in Canada by
SAUNDERS BOOK COMPANY
Collingwood, Ontario, Canada L9Y 3Z7
(800) 461-9120

Library of Congress Cataloging-in-Publication Data
Rotter, Charles.
Walruses / by Charles Rotter.
p.   cm.
Summary: Describes the physical characteristics and habits
of walruses and some of the dangers they face.
ISBN 0-89565-841-0
1. Walruses--Juvenile literature.   [1. Walruses.]   I. Title.
QL737.P62R68   1993   92-8410
599.74'7--dc20   CIP
                                                              AC

For Lian

You wouldn't want to brush these teeth three times a day! Luckily, you don't have to. They belong to a big animal called a *walrus*. The teeth are called *tusks*, just like the tusks on an elephant. Walrus tusks can grow up to three feet long.

A walrus uses its tusks in many different ways. It can use them as weapons when it fights, or it might use them to dig up food from the sea bottom. A walrus will even use its tusks to pull itself out of the water.

Like their close relatives, the seals and sea lions, walruses spend a lot of time in the ocean. They live along coastlines far to the north. This part of the world is called the *Arctic*. It is very cold in the Arctic. It gets so cold that the ocean is often covered with ice. But walruses don't seem to mind the cold. They often come out of the water and sit on top of the floating chunks of ice.

How does a walrus stay warm in the half-frozen sea? A walrus has almost no hair on its body to keep it warm. Instead, a walrus has a thick layer of fat, called *blubber*, under its skin. The blubber helps keep in heat, protecting the walrus from the icy cold.

While a walrus has almost no hair on its body, it does have hair on its face. These hairs, called *bristles*, make a walrus look like it has a moustache. A walrus's bristles are very sensitive to touch, just like a cat's whiskers. A walrus uses its bristles to find its way through murky water. It also uses its bristles to find food.

Walruses eat many different kinds of food. They like to snack on clams, starfish, and other animals that live in the mud on the sea bottom. They also eat octopuses and fish. A hungry walrus will even attack seals with its great tusks.

Most walruses live in different places at different times of the year. Walruses follow the edge of the sea ice. In the summer, the ice melts in the southern parts of the Arctic. The walruses head north, where temperatures are cooler and there is still ice on the sea. They often ride on chunks of ice drifting in the water. When fall comes, the temperature begins to drop and ice builds up again farther south. The walruses then head south, staying near the edge of the advancing ice.

Walruses gather in large groups called *herds*. The herd in this picture is gathered at Round Island, a place famous for its walrus herds. Round Island is located in the Bering Sea, off the coast of Alaska. Thousands of walruses gather there every year. Some older walruses on Round Island don't travel with the seasons. They stay there year-round, lounging in the sun.

Male walruses are called *bulls*. Bulls sometimes swell up their throats and make a sound just like a ringing bell. When a walrus makes this sound, scientists say that the walrus is "pinging." The pinging walrus may be warning its neighbors to stay away, or he might be trying to attract female walruses, called *cows*.

A walrus cow normally has one baby at a time. A young cow gives birth every two years. As the cow gets older, she gives birth less often. An older cow gives birth every three of four years, or even longer.

A young walrus, called a *calf*, is helpless without its mother. The cow takes care of her calf for a long time. She protects it and feeds it milk from her body. When the calf is about two years old, it can take care of itself and find its own food.

Walruses don't have many enemies, but the ones they do have can be very dangerous. Both killer whales and polar bears eat walruses. Killer whales can catch full-grown walruses that are in the water. A walrus may try to defend itself with its tusks, but a killer whale is bigger, stronger, and faster. Polar bears can catch only small walruses that are out of the water. They often catch calves that are resting on shore.

People also hunt and kill walruses. Some Eskimo people survive by hunting walruses. They use every part of the animals they kill. They eat the meat and use the skins to make boats. The Eskimos make tools from the walrus's tusks and bones.

Sadly, some people kill walruses just for their tusks. The tusks are made of ivory, and ivory is very valuable. It can be carved and made into many things. Over the past century, greedy ivory hunters have killed thousands of walruses. They killed so many that very few walruses were left.

Fortunately, laws were passed to protect the walrus. Though some hunters still kill walruses illegally, the number of walruses has steadily grown. Walruses are safe for now. As long as we're careful, walruses will continue to swim in the northern seas.

THE CHILD'S WORLD
NATUREBOOKS

Wildlife Library

Alligators	Musk-oxen
Arctic Foxes	Octopuses
Bald Eagles	Owls
Beavers	Penguins
Birds	Polar Bears
Black Widows	Primates
Camels	Rattlesnakes
Cheetahs	Reptiles
Coyotes	Rhinoceroses
Dogs	Seals and Sea Lions
Dolphins	Sharks
Elephants	Snakes
Fish	Spiders
Giraffes	Tigers
Insects	Walruses
Kangaroos	Whales
Lions	Wildcats
Mammals	Wolves
Monarchs	Zebras

Space Library

Earth	The Moon
Mars	The Sun

Adventure Library

Glacier National Park	Yellowstone National Park
The Grand Canyon	Yosemite